LOOK INSIDE
CROSS-SECTIONS
BULLDOZERS

THE NYACK LIBRARY
NYACK, N. Y. 10960

P9-ARV-929

LOOK INSIDE
CROSS-SECTIONS
BULLDOZERS

ILLUSTRATED BY
CHRIS LYON AND GARY BIGGIN

WRITTEN BY
MOIRA BUTTERFIELD

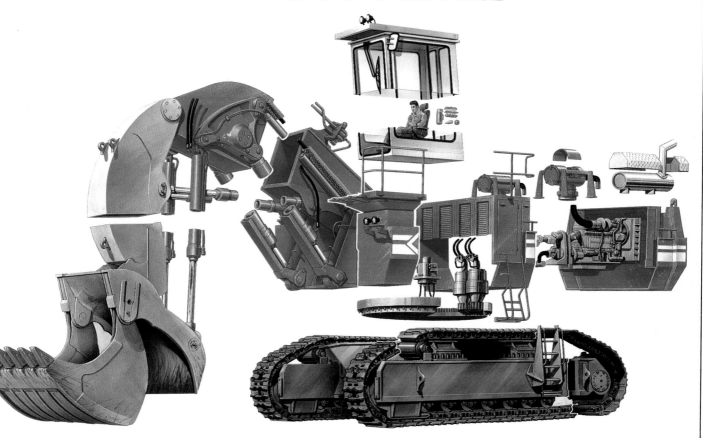

THE NYACK LIBRARY
NYACK, N. Y. 10960

DORLING KINDERSLEY
LONDON • NEW YORK • STUTTGART

A DORLING KINDERSLEY BOOK

Art Editor Dorian Spencer Davies
Designers Sharon Grant, Sara Hill
Senior Art Editor C. David Gillingwater
Project Editor Constance Novis
Senior Editor John C. Miles
U.S. Editor Camela Decaire
Production Louise Barratt
Consultants Leonard Butterfield
Charles Hunt

First American edition, 1995
2 4 6 8 10 9 7 5 3 1
Published in the United States
by Dorling Kindersley Publishing, Inc.,
95 Madison Avenue, New York, New York 10016

Copyright © 1995
Dorling Kindersley Limited, London

All rights reserved under International and Pan-American
Copyright Conventions. No part of this publication
may be reproduced, stored in a retrieval system,
or transmitted in any form or by any means,
electronic, mechanical, photocopying, recording
or otherwise, without the prior written
permission of the copyright owner. Published
in Great Britain by Dorling Kindersley Limited.
Distributed by Houghton Mifflin Company, Boston.

Library of Congress Cataloging - in - Publication Data

Bulldozers/author, Moira Butterfield;
artist, Christopher Lyon and Gary Biggin – 1st American ed.
p. cm. – (Look inside cross-sections)
Includes index.
ISBN 0-7894-0012-X
1. Bulldozers – Juvenile literature.
I. Lyon, Chris, ill.
II. Title. III. Series.
TA735. B88 1995

629. 225 – dc20   94 – 41309
                                     CIP
                                     AC

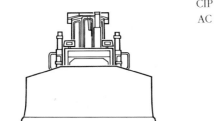

Reproduced by Dot Gradations, Essex
Printed and bound by Proost, Belgium

CONTENTS

WHEEL
LOADER
6-7

DUMP
TRUCK
8-9

MINING
SHOVEL
10-11

TRACK
PAVER
12-13

TRUCK
CRANE
14-15

CEMENT MIXER 16-17

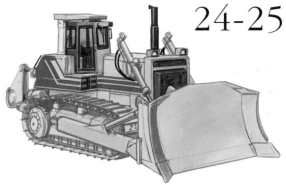

BULLDOZER 24-25

EXCAVATOR 18-19

SCRAPER 26-27

BACKHOE LOADER 20-21

HOW MACHINES WORK 28-29

SKID STEER 22

MINI-EXCAVATOR 23

GLOSSARY 30-31

INDEX 32

WHEEL LOADER

WHEREVER PEOPLE NEED TO DIG large holes or move heavy loads, you will see working vehicles such as trucks and diggers. By the time you finish this book, you will be at to recognize and name all kinds of those machines, including some even construction experts probably can't name! The vehicle on this page is called a wheel loader. It has a giant shovel called a bucket for scooping up loads, moving them, and filling up the back of dump trucks. Loaders are used at building sites and roadworks, mines, quarries, and garbage dumps, and are even lowered into ships' holds to help clear out cargoes such as coal.

Comfortable cab

The driver's cab is mounted up high so the driver can see all around. Inside, the controls are positioned within easy reach, so the driver doesn't tire while working. The cab is soundproofed and designed so that it does not shake as the loader does its job.

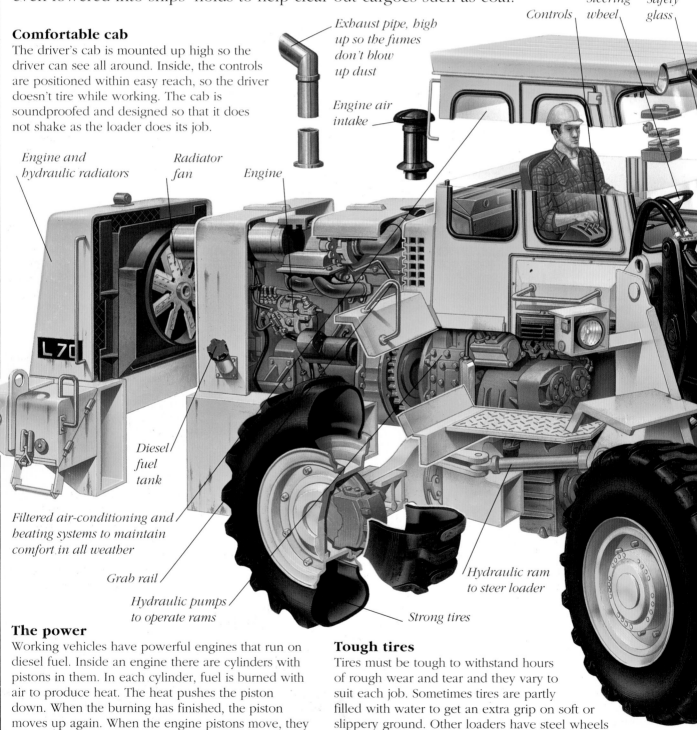

Steering wheel

Safety glass

Controls

Exhaust pipe, high up so the fumes don't blow up dust

Engine air intake

Engine and hydraulic radiators

Radiator fan

Engine

Diesel fuel tank

Filtered air-conditioning and heating systems to maintain comfort in all weather

Grab rail

Hydraulic pumps to operate rams

Hydraulic ram to steer loader

Strong tires

The power

Working vehicles have powerful engines that run on diesel fuel. Inside an engine there are cylinders with pistons in them. In each cylinder, fuel is burned with air to produce heat. The heat pushes the piston down. When the burning has finished, the piston moves up again. When the engine pistons move, they provide power for all the vehicle's working parts.

Tough tires

Tires must be tough to withstand hours of rough wear and tear and they vary to suit each job. Sometimes tires are partly filled with water to get an extra grip on soft or slippery ground. Other loaders have steel wheels that help spread and press down loose surfaces.

TECHNICAL DATA

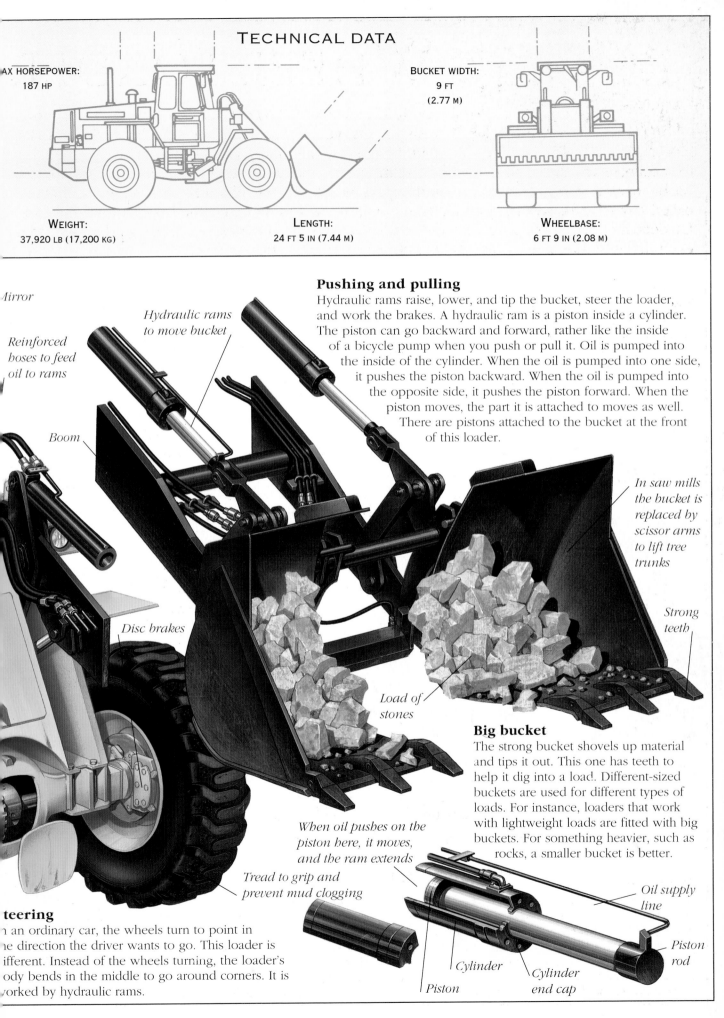

AX HORSEPOWER:
187 HP

BUCKET WIDTH:
9 FT
(2.77 M)

WEIGHT:
37,920 LB (17,200 KG)

LENGTH:
24 FT 5 IN (7.44 M)

WHEELBASE:
6 FT 9 IN (2.08 M)

Mirror

Reinforced hoses to feed oil to rams

Hydraulic rams to move bucket

Boom

Disc brakes

Pushing and pulling

Hydraulic rams raise, lower, and tip the bucket, steer the loader, and work the brakes. A hydraulic ram is a piston inside a cylinder. The piston can go backward and forward, rather like the inside of a bicycle pump when you push or pull it. Oil is pumped into the inside of the cylinder. When the oil is pumped into one side, it pushes the piston backward. When the oil is pumped into the opposite side, it pushes the piston forward. When the piston moves, the part it is attached to moves as well. There are pistons attached to the bucket at the front of this loader.

In saw mills the bucket is replaced by scissor arms to lift tree trunks

Strong teeth

Load of stones

Big bucket

The strong bucket shovels up material and tips it out. This one has teeth to help it dig into a load. Different-sized buckets are used for different types of loads. For instance, loaders that work with lightweight loads are fitted with big buckets. For something heavier, such as rocks, a smaller bucket is better.

When oil pushes on the piston here, it moves, and the ram extends

Tread to grip and prevent mud clogging

Oil supply line

Piston rod

Cylinder

Cylinder end cap

Piston

teering

n an ordinary car, the wheels turn to point in e direction the driver wants to go. This loader is ifferent. Instead of the wheels turning, the loader's ody bends in the middle to go around corners. It is orked by hydraulic rams.

DUMP TRUCK

DUMP TRUCKS CARRY HEAVY LOADS such as rocks and earth and work on construction sites and at quarries. The bigger the truck, the heavier the load it can carry. Some dump trucks are as tall as a house and can carry loads of more than 100 tons. On the back of a dump truck is the tipping body, specially reinforced, shaped, and even heated so it can carry loads in all kinds of weather. It tilts up to make a load spill out.

Tipping up

The tipping body is pushed up or pulled down by hydraulic rams (see page 7). The steel floor is extra thick to withstand wear and tear. It is a shallow V-shape with the back end sloped so that a load slides out easily in a funnel shape.

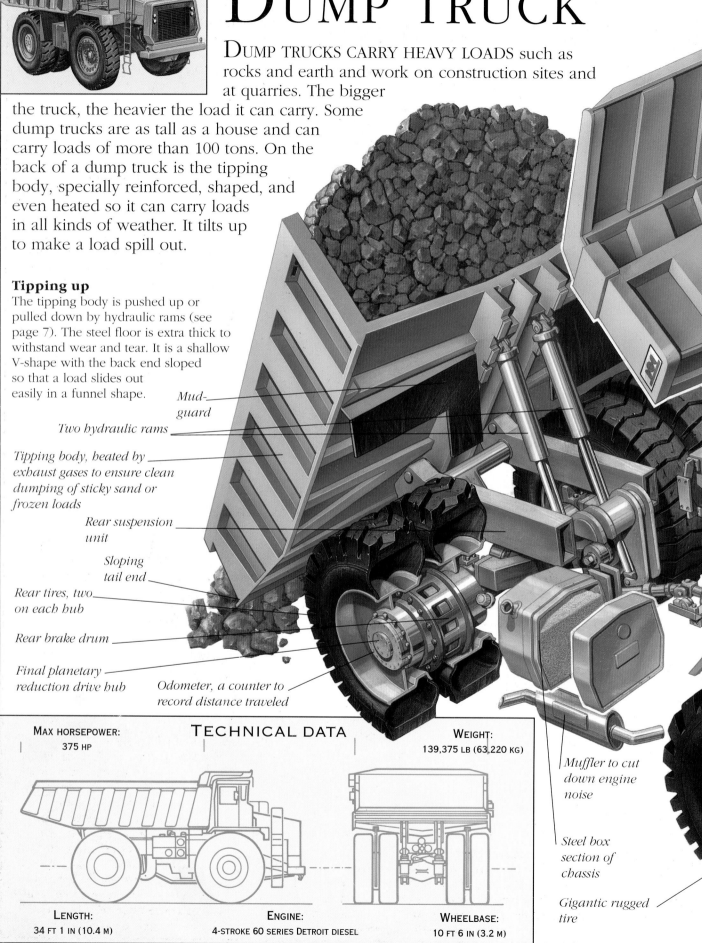

Mud-guard

Two hydraulic rams

Tipping body, heated by exhaust gases to ensure clean dumping of sticky sand or frozen loads

Rear suspension unit

Sloping tail end

Rear tires, two on each hub

Rear brake drum

Final planetary reduction drive hub

Odometer, a counter to record distance traveled

Muffler to cut down engine noise

Steel box section of chassis

Gigantic rugged tire

TECHNICAL DATA

MAX HORSEPOWER:
375 HP

WEIGHT:
139,375 LB (63,220 KG)

LENGTH:
34 FT 1 IN (10.4 M)

ENGINE:
4-STROKE 60 SERIES DETROIT DIESEL

WHEELBASE:
10 FT 6 IN (3.2 M)

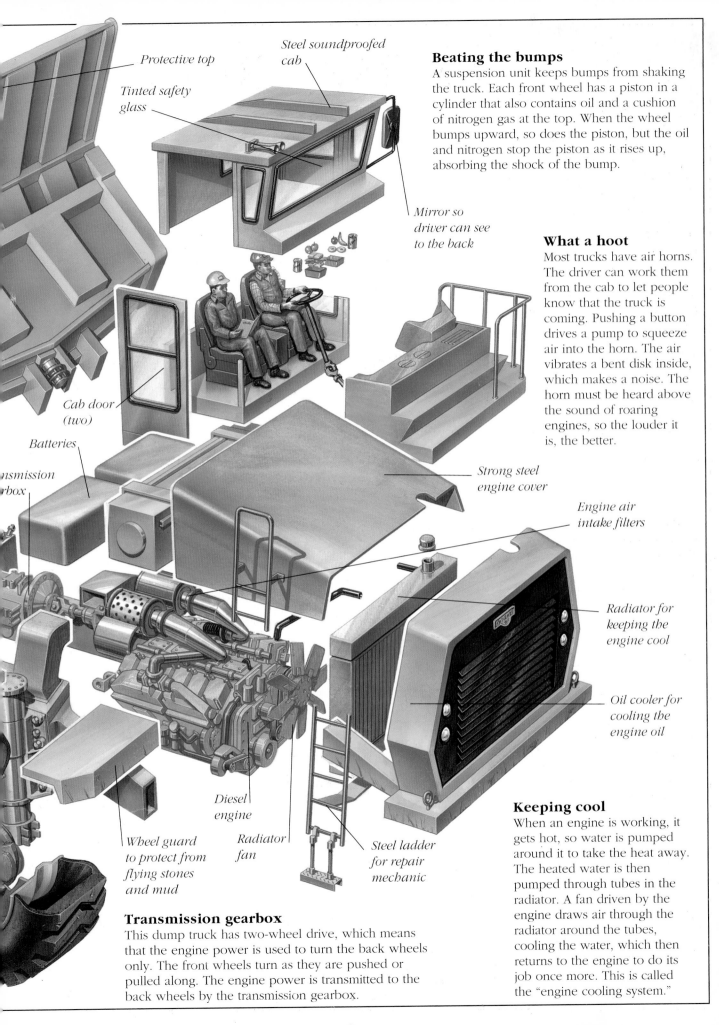

Protective top

Steel soundproofed
cab

Tinted safety
glass

Beating the bumps
A suspension unit keeps bumps from shaking
the truck. Each front wheel has a piston in a
cylinder that also contains oil and a cushion
of nitrogen gas at the top. When the wheel
bumps upward, so does the piston, but the oil
and nitrogen stop the piston as it rises up,
absorbing the shock of the bump.

Mirror so
driver can see
to the back

What a hoot
Most trucks have air horns.
The driver can work them
from the cab to let people
know that the truck is
coming. Pushing a button
drives a pump to squeeze
air into the horn. The air
vibrates a bent disk inside,
which makes a noise. The
horn must be heard above
the sound of roaring
engines, so the louder it
is, the better.

Cab door
(two)

Batteries

nsmission
rbox

Strong steel
engine cover

Engine air
intake filters

Radiator for
keeping the
engine cool

Oil cooler for
cooling the
engine oil

Diesel
engine

Wheel guard
to protect from
flying stones
and mud

Radiator
fan

Steel ladder
for repair
mechanic

Keeping cool
When an engine is working, it
gets hot, so water is pumped
around it to take the heat away.
The heated water is then
pumped through tubes in the
radiator. A fan driven by the
engine draws air through the
radiator around the tubes,
cooling the water, which then
returns to the engine to do its
job once more. This is called
the "engine cooling system."

Transmission gearbox
This dump truck has two-wheel drive, which means
that the engine power is used to turn the back wheels
only. The front wheels turn as they are pushed or
pulled along. The engine power is transmitted to the
back wheels by the transmission gearbox.

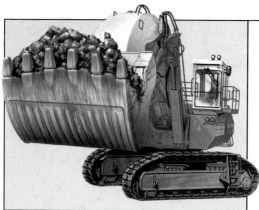

MINING SHOVEL

THIS MONSTER MACHINE CUTS AWAY SEAMS OF COAL o_ shale from the walls of opencut mines. Its massive bucket is _ fitted with strong teeth that bite upward into the coal or rock in front of them. When the bucket is full, the driver swings t_ top of the machine around and opens the back of the bucke_ to drop the load into a dump truck. The shovel shown here _ can fill the back of a 130-ton dump truck in just two minutes! Mining shovels can be fitted with a computer monitoring system. On some systems the computer automatically shuts off the engine if there is any danger of a breakdown.

Super scooper

The bucket is worked by hydraulic rams. It is hinged in the middle so the back can open and close. The giant metal teeth are shaped so that they stay sharp as they work, but when they eventually wear out, they can easily be replaced.

Mining giants

This machine is small compared to some versions. Very large mining shovels can weigh up to 530 tons, the weight of about 85 big elephants! Some supersized machines have six to eight buckets fixed on a giant wheel that turns around as the shovel moves along a rock face. Models of this size can be run by computers instead of human drivers.

Breakdown backup

The shovel must be very reliable. If it stopped working, production in the mine would stop and its owners would lose lots of money. To prevent this, it has two diesel engines. It can work on just one if the other breaks down. It also has an automatic system that keeps all its vital parts lubricated.

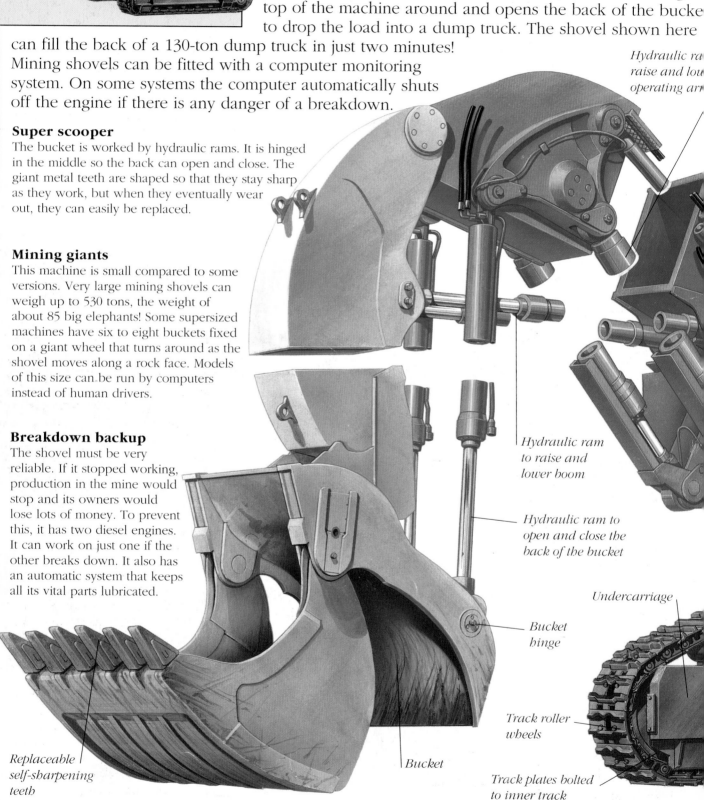

*Hydraulic ra_
raise and lo_
operating ar_*

*Hydraulic ram
to raise and
lower boom*

*Hydraulic ram to
open and close the
back of the bucket*

Undercarriage

*Bucket
hinge*

*Track roller
wheels*

Bucket

*Replaceable
self-sharpening
teeth*

*Track plates bolted
to inner track*

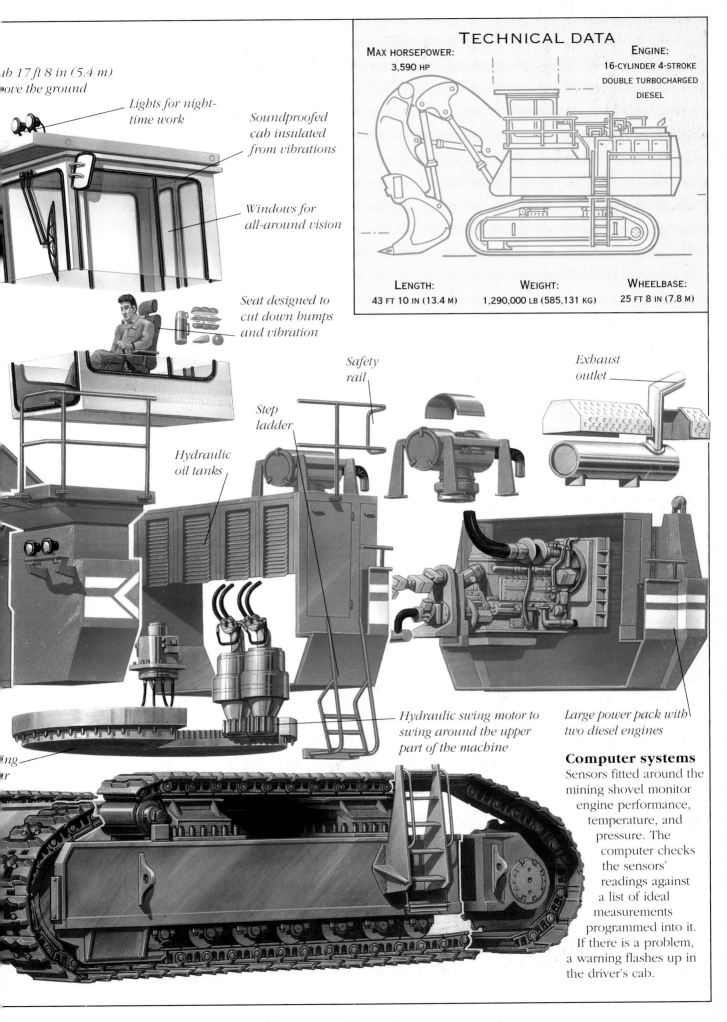

ab 17 ft 8 in (5.4 m)
ove the ground

Lights for night-
time work

Soundproofed
cab insulated
from vibrations

Windows for
all-around vision

Seat designed to
cut down bumps
and vibration

Safety
rail

Step
ladder

Exhaust
outlet

Hydraulic
oil tanks

ng
r

Hydraulic swing motor to
swing around the upper
part of the machine

Large power pack with
two diesel engines

TECHNICAL DATA

MAX HORSEPOWER:	ENGINE:
3,590 HP	16-CYLINDER 4-STROKE DOUBLE TURBOCHARGED DIESEL

LENGTH:	WEIGHT:	WHEELBASE:
43 FT 10 IN (13.4 M)	1,290,000 LB (585,131 KG)	25 FT 8 IN (7.8 M)

Computer systems

Sensors fitted around the mining shovel monitor engine performance, temperature, and pressure. The computer checks the sensors' readings against a list of ideal measurements programmed into it. If there is a problem, a warning flashes up in the driver's cab.

TRACK PAVER

THIS BIG CUMBERSOME MACHINE has one of the hottest, smelliest, noisiest jobs featured in this book! It lays down a mixture of tar and crushed rocks on new roads or resurfaces ones. The mixture is loaded into the front of the paver; then it passes through the machine and gets dropped onto the road. It is spread out by giant corkscrews, called augers, and then smoothed flat by heated plates – just like warm butter spread onto bread!

Spreading it wide

If the driver wants to heat and smooth a surface that is wider than the paver itself, screed plates that extend out to the sides of the paver can be used. At the back of the paver there are "footplates" where workers can stand. They might want to hop off and even up the path surface and edges with their rakes. They wear protective boots that get very sticky and tar-covered as they work!

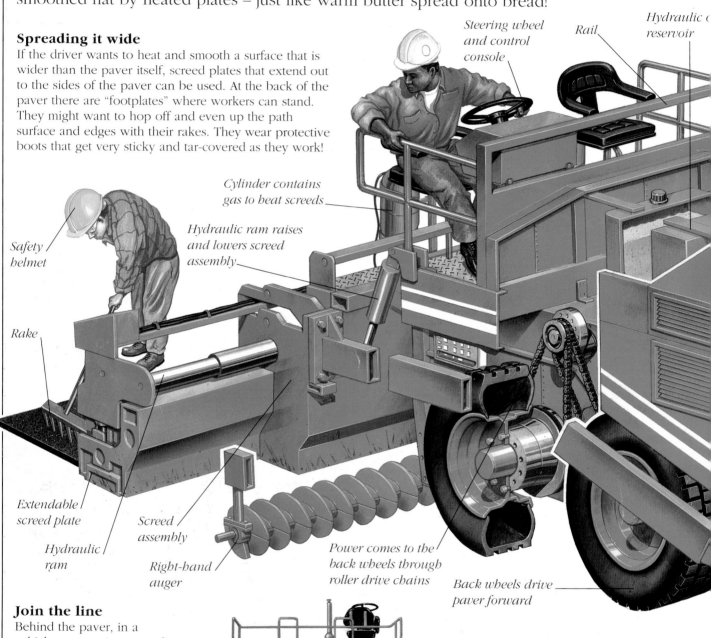

Steering wheel and control console

Rail

Hydraulic reservoir

Cylinder contains gas to heat screeds

Hydraulic ram raises and lowers screed assembly

Safety helmet

Rake

Extendable screed plate

Hydraulic ram

Screed assembly

Right-hand auger

Power comes to the back wheels through roller drive chains

Back wheels drive paver forward

Join the line

Behind the paver, in a vehicle convoy, is a spreading vehicle that lays a mixture of tar and larger stones on the new surface. Behind that is a heavy roller vehicle that pushes the large stones into the soft surface laid by the paver.

Extendable screed plate

Footplate

Look both ways

The driver regularly swaps seating positions between the left and right to check what's happening on both sides as the new surface is being l. There is a brake pedal under each seat, and the steering wheel and control console can slide from left right on a rail in front of the driver.

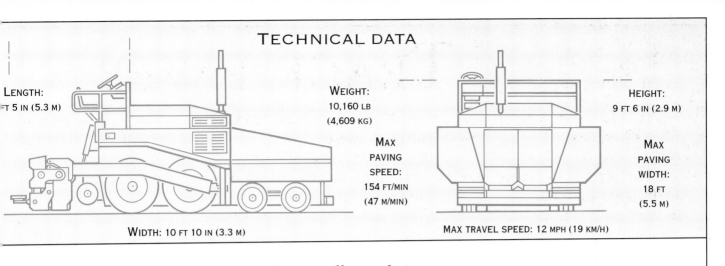

TECHNICAL DATA

LENGTH:
FT 5 IN (5.3 M)

WEIGHT:
10,160 LB
(4,609 KG)

MAX PAVING SPEED:
154 FT/MIN
(47 M/MIN)

HEIGHT:
9 FT 6 IN (2.9 M)

MAX PAVING WIDTH:
18 FT
(5.5 M)

WIDTH: 10 FT 10 IN (3.3 M)

MAX TRAVEL SPEED: 12 MPH (19 KM/H)

Stop smelly smoke!

Like all the working vehicles in this book, the paver has a diesel engine that burns diesel fuel and air. This creates gases, some of which go out through the exhaust pipe. If the engine is maintained properly, the exhaust fumes pollute the air as little as possible. But if a vehicle starts pouring out blue or black exhaust smoke, it means something is wrong – the engine parts may be wearing out or be adjusted incorrectly.

Going under

Conveyors called feeders carry the tar and stone mixture toward the back of the paver, where it drops onto the road. Then, as the paver moves forward, giant augers rotate around, spreading the mixture out over the road surface. As the paver continues to move forward, the heated screed plates smooth the new surface to the correct thickness.

Up front

At the front of the vehicle convoy is a dump truck filled with mixed tar and crushed rock. The truck dumps this into the hopper at the front of the paver. The truck and paver move forward together so the paver can be continually reloaded as it lays the new surface on a road.

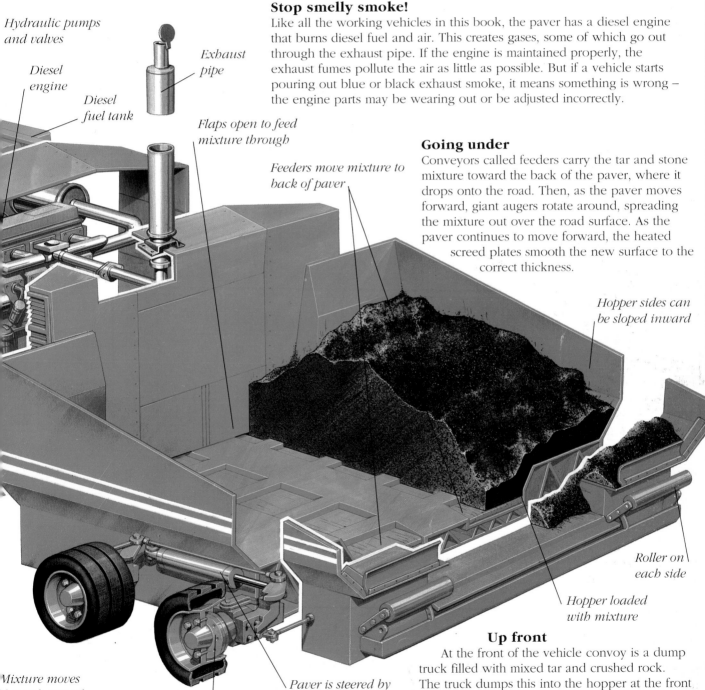

Hydraulic pumps and valves

Diesel engine

Exhaust pipe

Diesel fuel tank

Flaps open to feed mixture through

Feeders move mixture to back of paver

Hopper sides can be sloped inward

Roller on each side

Hopper loaded with mixture

Mixture moves through tunnel

Paver is steered by moving the front wheels

Hub

TRUCK CRANE

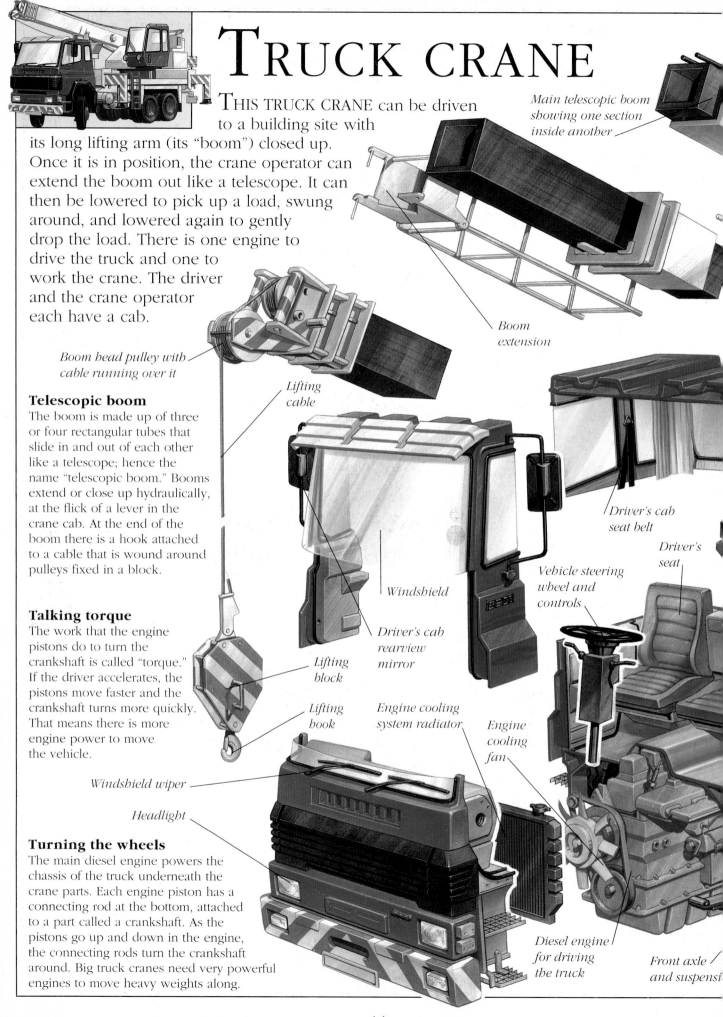

THIS TRUCK CRANE can be driven to a building site with its long lifting arm (its "boom") closed up. Once it is in position, the crane operator can extend the boom out like a telescope. It can then be lowered to pick up a load, swung around, and lowered again to gently drop the load. There is one engine to drive the truck and one to work the crane. The driver and the crane operator each have a cab.

Main telescopic boom showing one section inside another

Boom extension

Boom head pulley with cable running over it

Lifting cable

Telescopic boom

The boom is made up of three or four rectangular tubes that slide in and out of each other like a telescope; hence the name "telescopic boom." Booms extend or close up hydraulically, at the flick of a lever in the crane cab. At the end of the boom there is a hook attached to a cable that is wound around pulleys fixed in a block.

Talking torque

The work that the engine pistons do to turn the crankshaft is called "torque." If the driver accelerates, the pistons move faster and the crankshaft turns more quickly. That means there is more engine power to move the vehicle.

Lifting block

Lifting hook

Windshield wiper

Headlight

Windshield

Driver's cab rearview mirror

Engine cooling system radiator

Engine cooling fan

Driver's cab seat belt

Driver's seat

Vehicle steering wheel and controls

Turning the wheels

The main diesel engine powers the chassis of the truck underneath the crane parts. Each engine piston has a connecting rod at the bottom, attached to a part called a crankshaft. As the pistons go up and down in the engine, the connecting rods turn the crankshaft around. Big truck cranes need very powerful engines to move heavy weights along.

Diesel engine for driving the truck

Front axle and suspensi

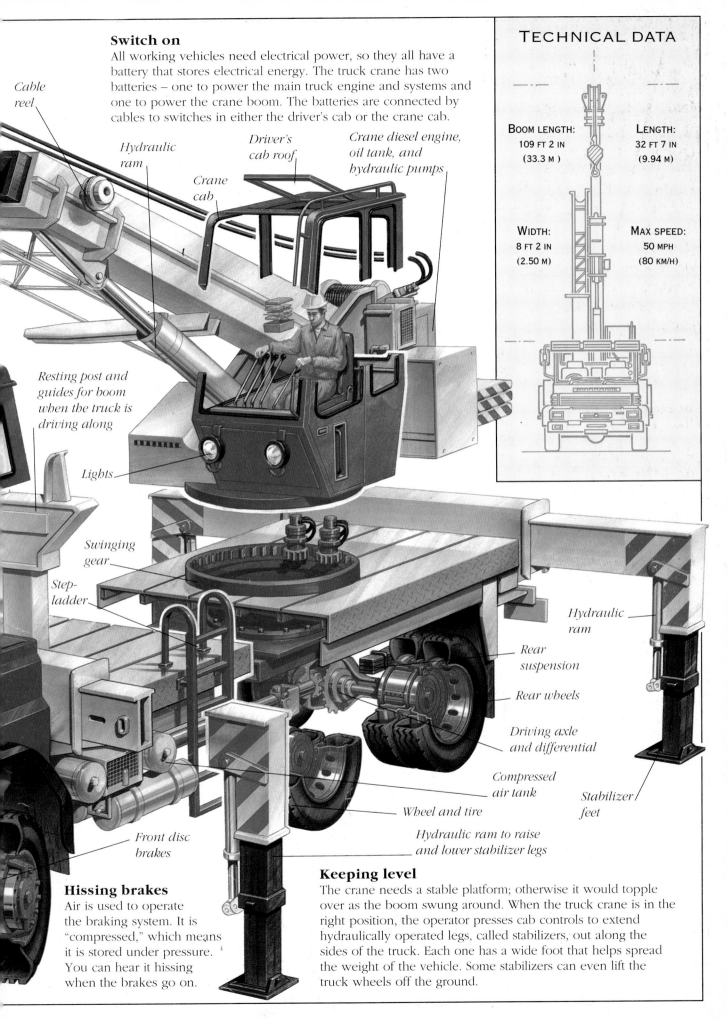

Switch on

All working vehicles need electrical power, so they all have a battery that stores electrical energy. The truck crane has two batteries – one to power the main truck engine and systems and one to power the crane boom. The batteries are connected by cables to switches in either the driver's cab or the crane cab.

Cable reel

Hydraulic ram

Driver's cab roof

Crane diesel engine, oil tank, and hydraulic pumps

Crane cab

Resting post and guides for boom when the truck is driving along

Lights

Swinging gear

Step-ladder

Front disc brakes

Rear suspension

Rear wheels

Driving axle and differential

Compressed air tank

Wheel and tire

Hydraulic ram

Stabilizer feet

Hydraulic ram to raise and lower stabilizer legs

TECHNICAL DATA

BOOM LENGTH:	LENGTH:
109 FT 2 IN	32 FT 7 IN
(33.3 M)	(9.94 M)

WIDTH:	MAX SPEED:
8 FT 2 IN	50 MPH
(2.50 M)	(80 KM/H)

Hissing brakes

Air is used to operate the braking system. It is "compressed," which means it is stored under pressure. You can hear it hissing when the brakes go on.

Keeping level

The crane needs a stable platform; otherwise it would topple over as the boom swung around. When the truck crane is in the right position, the operator presses cab controls to extend hydraulically operated legs, called stabilizers, out along the sides of the truck. Each one has a wide foot that helps spread the weight of the vehicle. Some stabilizers can even lift the truck wheels off the ground.

CEMENT MIXER

A CEMENT MIXER CAN GO AROUND and forward at the same ti
As it drives, its giant drum mixes the cement loaded inside it, read
spreading when it arrives at a building site. If the cement needs to
an inaccessible area, workers can fit a conve
running from the back of the mixer pouri
chute.

Down and out

The materials used to make
the cement are loaded into the
drum through the hopper. Sand
and crushed rocks are usually
the main ingredients. Mixed
cement comes out through
a chute that can be directed
straight down or to the sides.

Inside the drum

Just before the mixer gets to
its destination the driver can
operate controls to pump
water into the drum and start
it turning. Welded inside the
drum are giant blades called
flights, fitted in a spiral pattern.
They push the mixture to the
front or the back of the drum,
depending on which direction
the driver rotates the drum.

Hopper

*Ladder to get
to the hopper*

*Conveyor delivers
cement away
from truck*

*Cement mixture
coming down the
chute*

*Flights inside
drum*

*Conveyor
attachment controls*

*Levers for controlling the
operation of the drum*

Drum drive

This mixer has one engine that drives
the wheels and turns the drum. Some
mixers have two engines – one for the wheels
and one for the drum. If you see a drum going around
faster than usual, it is probably being turned quickly to
mix dry ingredients together inside before water is added.

*Operator controlling
the cement discharge
from the drum*

16

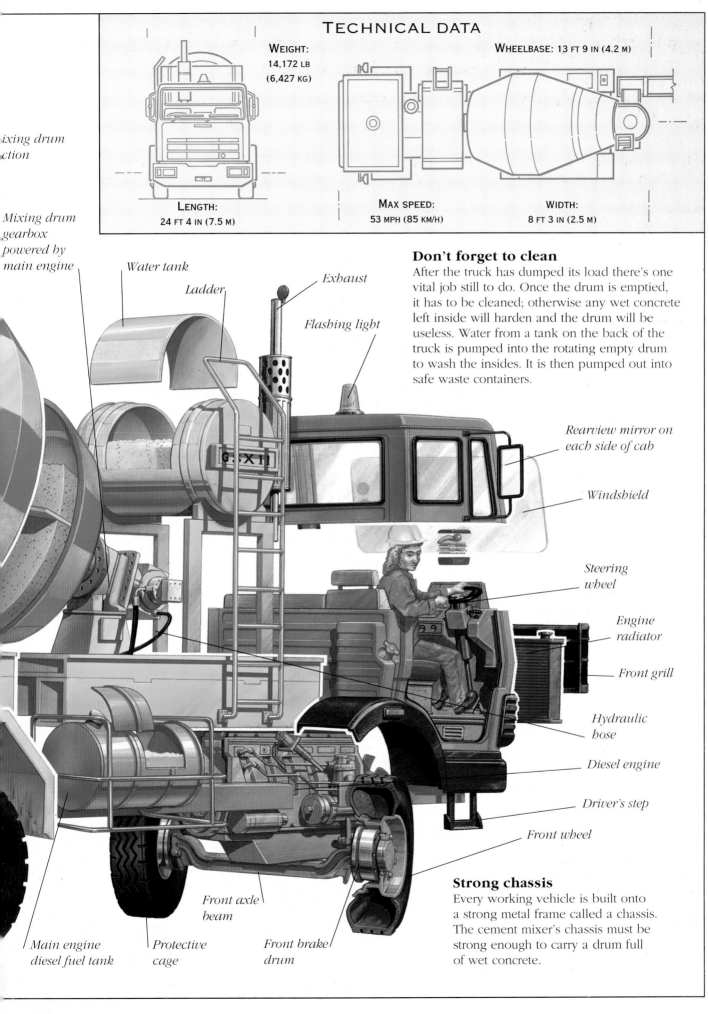

WEIGHT:
14,172 LB
(6,427 KG)

WHEELBASE: 13 FT 9 IN (4.2 M)

LENGTH:
24 FT 4 IN (7.5 M)

MAX SPEED:
53 MPH (85 KM/H)

WIDTH:
8 FT 3 IN (2.5 M)

ixing drum
ction

Mixing drum
gearbox
powered by
main engine

Water tank

Ladder

Exhaust

Flashing light

Don't forget to clean

After the truck has dumped its load there's one
vital job still to do. Once the drum is emptied,
it has to be cleaned; otherwise any wet concrete
left inside will harden and the drum will be
useless. Water from a tank on the back of the
truck is pumped into the rotating empty drum
to wash the insides. It is then pumped out into
safe waste containers.

Rearview mirror on
each side of cab

Windshield

Steering
wheel

Engine
radiator

Front grill

Hydraulic
hose

Diesel engine

Driver's step

Front wheel

Strong chassis

Every working vehicle is built onto
a strong metal frame called a chassis.
The cement mixer's chassis must be
strong enough to carry a drum full
of wet concrete.

Main engine
diesel fuel tank

Protective
cage

Front brake
drum

Front axle
beam

EXCAVATOR

NEXT TIME YOU ARE IN A CAR that drives by some roadwork, look out f
a wheeled excavator busy digging a hole or a trench, or picking up a load
earth and stones. You might also see one working hard on a building site.
If you live in a modern house, a wheeled excavator probably helped dig th
foundations.

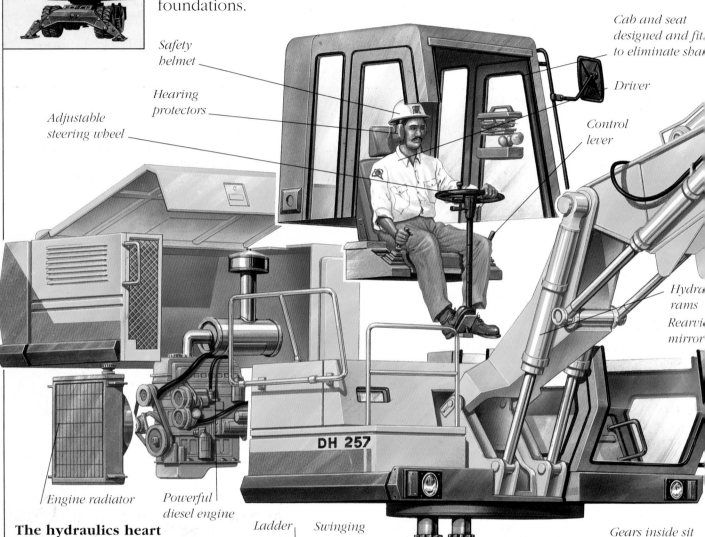

Safety
helmet

Hearing
protectors

Adjustable
steering wheel

Cab and seat
designed and fit.
to eliminate sha

Driver

Control
lever

Hydra
rams
Rearvi
mirror

Engine radiator

Powerful
diesel engine

DH 257

The hydraulics heart

The hydraulic power pack contains all
the hydraulic oil pumps and control valves
that the driver operates with the levers
inside the cab. Hydraulic oil is pumped
from here to all the different rams that
make the machine dig and lift.

Swinging cab

The driver can swing the cab around
to operate the grabber in a new
position using a gear called the
"swinging gear." This is used for picking
up a load and swinging it around to
dump it onto the back of a truck. When
the excavator is driving along, the
swinging gear is locked so the
cab won't move accidentally.

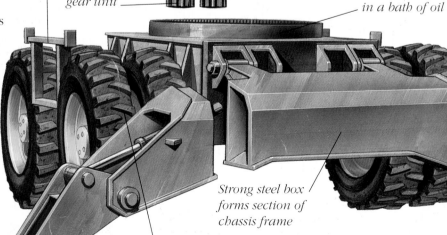

Ladder

Swinging
gear unit

Gears inside sit
in a bath of oil

Strong steel box
forms section of
chassis frame

Rugged heavy-
duty tires

Tread pattern designed to grip well
and keep tires from clogging with n

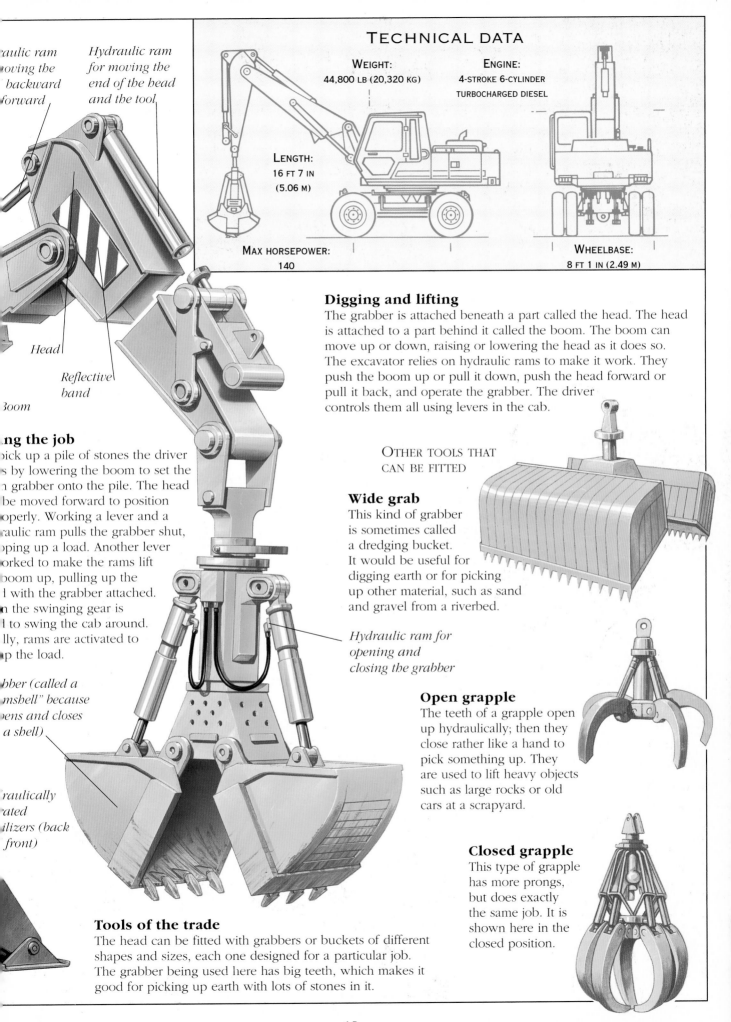

raulic ram
oving the
backward
forward

*Hydraulic ram
for moving the
end of the head
and the tool*

Head

*Reflective
band*

Boom

ng the job

ick up a pile of stones the driver
s by lowering the boom to set the
grabber onto the pile. The head
be moved forward to position
operly. Working a lever and a
raulic ram pulls the grabber shut,
ping up a load. Another lever
orked to make the rams lift
boom up, pulling up the
I with the grabber attached.
n the swinging gear is
I to swing the cab around.
lly, rams are activated to
p the load.

*bber (called a
mshell" because
ens and closes
a shell)*

*raulically
rated
ilizers (back
front)*

Tools of the trade

The head can be fitted with grabbers or buckets of different
shapes and sizes, each one designed for a particular job.
The grabber being used here has big teeth, which makes it
good for picking up earth with lots of stones in it.

TECHNICAL DATA

WEIGHT:
44,800 LB (20,320 KG)

ENGINE:
4-STROKE 6-CYLINDER
TURBOCHARGED DIESEL

LENGTH:
16 FT 7 IN
(5.06 M)

MAX HORSEPOWER:
140

WHEELBASE:
8 FT 1 IN (2.49 M)

Digging and lifting

The grabber is attached beneath a part called the head. The head
is attached to a part behind it called the boom. The boom can
move up or down, raising or lowering the head as it does so.
The excavator relies on hydraulic rams to make it work. They
push the boom up or pull it down, push the head forward or
pull it back, and operate the grabber. The driver
controls them all using levers in the cab.

OTHER TOOLS THAT
CAN BE FITTED

Wide grab

This kind of grabber
is sometimes called
a dredging bucket.
It would be useful for
digging earth or for picking
up other material, such as sand
and gravel from a riverbed.

*Hydraulic ram for
opening and
closing the grabber*

Open grapple

The teeth of a grapple open
up hydraulically; then they
close rather like a hand to
pick something up. They
are used to lift heavy objects
such as large rocks or old
cars at a scrapyard.

Closed grapple

This type of grapple
has more prongs,
but does exactly
the same job. It is
shown here in the
closed position.

BACKHOE LOADER

LOOK OUT FOR BACKHOE LOADERS BUSY digging trenches, mov earth, or clearing ditches. If you are unlucky, you might even get st behind one in a traffic jam! Loaders are allowed to drive along the road, but only very slowly. But you could pass the time in the traffic jam figuring out which attachments are fitted to the loader in front of you. Look at the back to see if it has the backhoe shown here. As you finally go past, look at the front to see if has a loading bucket or some forklift equipment.

The backhoe

The backhoe is a long attachment that can be fitted behind the loader. It is made up of hydraulic arms with a bucket on the end, and it gets its name because of the way it works – it digs downward and pulls inward toward the back of the loader.

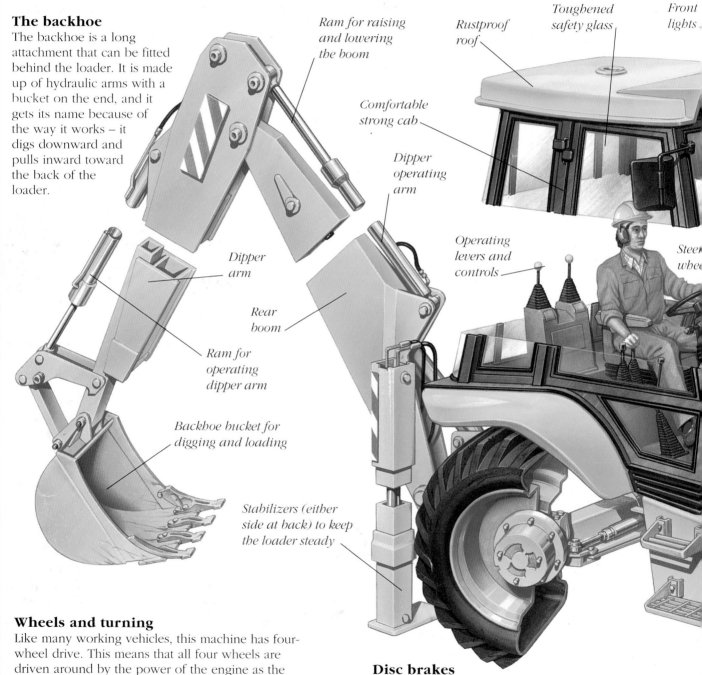

Ram for raising and lowering the boom

Rustproof roof

Toughened safety glass

Front lights

Comfortable strong cab

Dipper operating arm

Dipper arm

Rear boom

Operating levers and controls

Stee whee

Ram for operating dipper arm

Backhoe bucket for digging and loading

Stabilizers (either side at back) to keep the loader steady

Wheels and turning

Like many working vehicles, this machine has four-wheel drive. This means that all four wheels are driven around by the power of the engine as the loader goes along. On this model the driver can flick a switch to make the loader wheels steer in different ways. For instance, all four wheels can turn the same way, or the back and front wheels can turn different ways, or the two front wheels can turn on their own.

Disc brakes

There are disc brakes on this machine. A disc brake is a ca iron disk mounted on a wheel axle. The axle, the wheel, a the disk spin around together. The disk is sandwiched between two pads or plates that squeeze it and slow it do when the driver works the brake pedal.

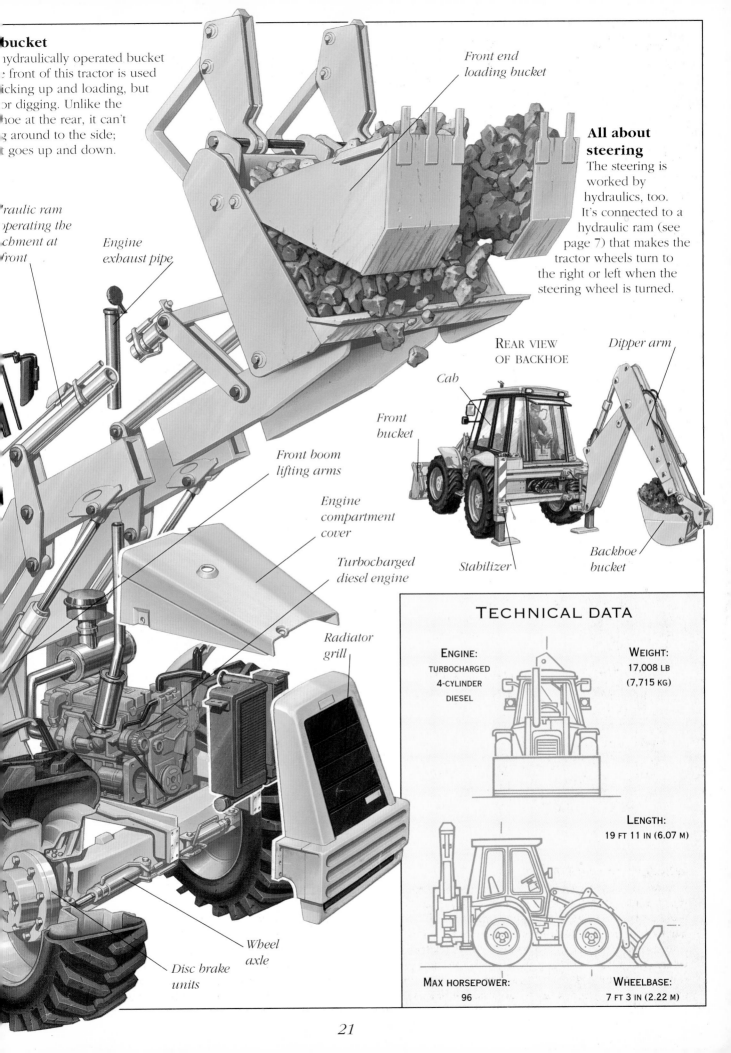

bucket

hydraulically operated bucket
e front of this tractor is used
cking up and loading, but
or digging. Unlike the
hoe at the rear, it can't
g around to the side;
goes up and down.

raulic ram
operating the
chment at
ront

Engine
exhaust pipe

Front end
loading bucket

All about steering
The steering is
worked by
hydraulics, too.
It's connected to a
hydraulic ram (see
page 7) that makes the
tractor wheels turn to
the right or left when the
steering wheel is turned.

REAR VIEW
OF BACKHOE

Dipper arm

Cab

Front
bucket

Front boom
lifting arms

Engine
compartment
cover

Turbocharged
diesel engine

Stabilizer

Backhoe
bucket

Radiator
grill

Wheel
axle

Disc brake
units

TECHNICAL DATA

ENGINE:
TURBOCHARGED
4-CYLINDER
DIESEL

WEIGHT:
17,008 LB
(7,715 KG)

LENGTH:
19 FT 11 IN (6.07 M)

MAX HORSEPOWER:
96

WHEELBASE:
7 FT 3 IN (2.22 M)

SKID STEER

DIGGING, LIFTING, LOADING, SWEEPING, RAKING – you name it, the skid steer can do it. It is so maneuverable and versatile it has even been to perform mechanical ballets! The secret is in the wheels. It turns by stopping both wheels on one side and spinning around on them, driven by the other two whe. The driver can even make the wheels on one side go forward while those on the other side go backward. Because it is able to turn quickly in a confined space, it is good for working in small areas, such as barns and farmyards.

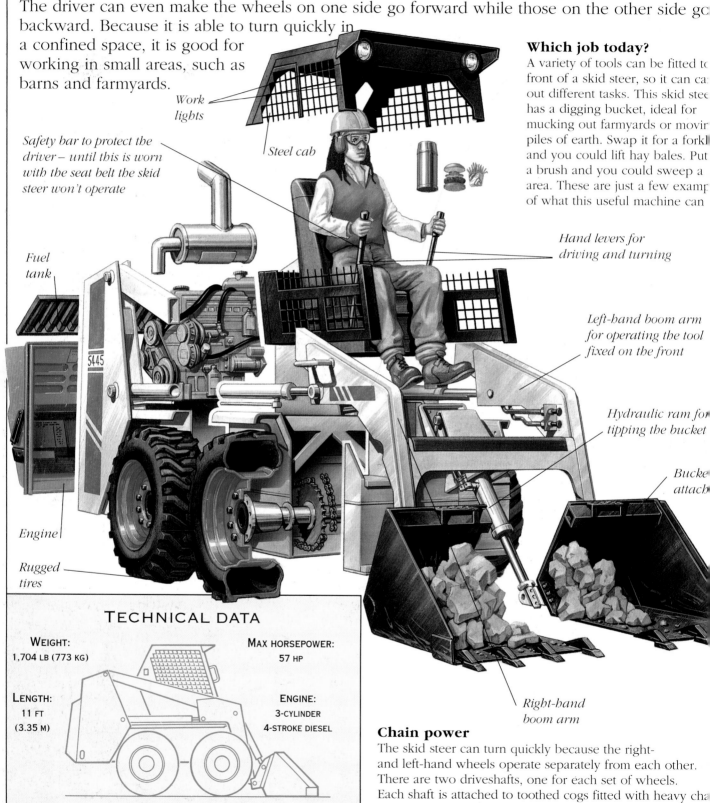

Work lights

Safety bar to protect the driver – until this is worn with the seat belt the skid steer won't operate

Steel cab

Fuel tank

5445

Engine

Rugged tires

Which job today?

A variety of tools can be fitted to front of a skid steer, so it can ca out different tasks. This skid stee has a digging bucket, ideal for mucking out farmyards or movir piles of earth. Swap it for a forkl and you could lift hay bales. Put a brush and you could sweep a area. These are just a few examp of what this useful machine can

Hand levers for driving and turning

Left-hand boom arm for operating the tool fixed on the front

Hydraulic ram for tipping the bucket

Bucke attach

Right-hand boom arm

Chain power

The skid steer can turn quickly because the right- and left-hand wheels operate separately from each other. There are two driveshafts, one for each set of wheels. Each shaft is attached to toothed cogs fitted with heavy cha

TECHNICAL DATA

WEIGHT:	MAX HORSEPOWER:
1,704 LB (773 KG)	57 HP

LENGTH:	ENGINE:
11 FT	3-CYLINDER
(3.35 M)	4-STROKE DIESEL

WHEELBASE: 3 FT 2 IN (.99 M)

MINI-EXCAVATOR

SOME WORKING MACHINES ARE BUILT MINI-SIZED to get into tight corners that big machines could never reach. This mini-excavator is not very wide and it can turn around in a very small space. It is often used for digging trenches to lay cables and pipes, so you might see one at a small roadwork site.

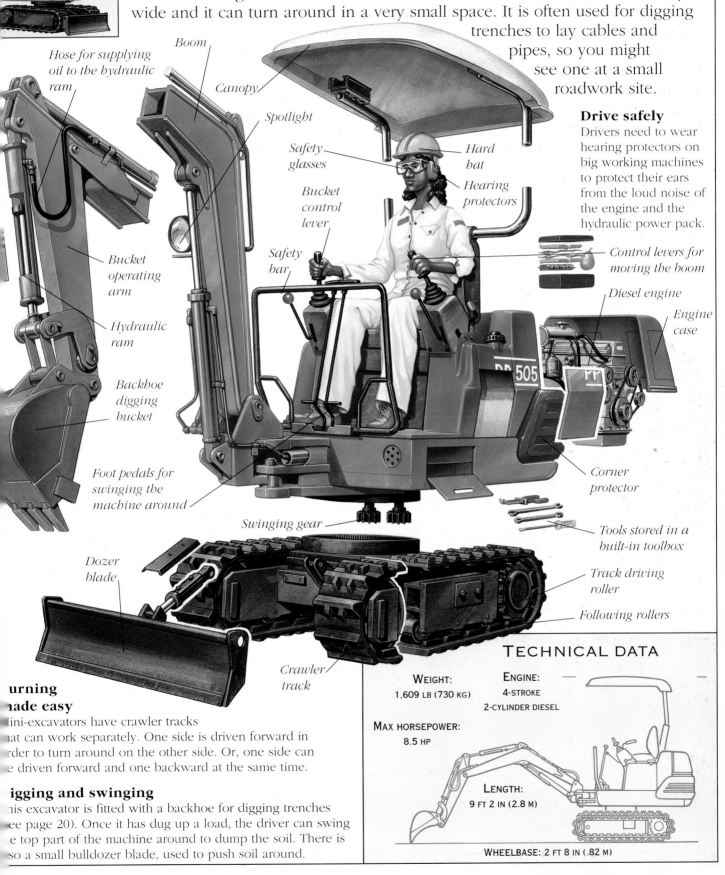

Hose for supplying oil to the hydraulic ram

Boom

Canopy

Spotlight

Safety glasses

Bucket control lever

Hard hat

Hearing protectors

Safety bar

Bucket operating arm

Hydraulic ram

Backhoe digging bucket

Foot pedals for swinging the machine around

Swinging gear

Dozer blade

Crawler track

Corner protector

Control levers for moving the boom

Diesel engine

Engine case

Tools stored in a built-in toolbox

Track driving roller

Following rollers

Drive safely
Drivers need to wear hearing protectors on big working machines to protect their ears from the loud noise of the engine and the hydraulic power pack.

[T]urning [m]ade easy
[M]ini-excavators have crawler tracks [th]at can work separately. One side is driven forward in [o]rder to turn around on the other side. Or, one side can [b]e driven forward and one backward at the same time.

[D]igging and swinging
[Th]is excavator is fitted with a backhoe for digging trenches [(s]ee page 20). Once it has dug up a load, the driver can swing [th]e top part of the machine around to dump the soil. There is [al]so a small bulldozer blade, used to push soil around.

TECHNICAL DATA

WEIGHT:
1,609 LB (730 KG)

ENGINE:
4-STROKE
2-CYLINDER DIESEL

MAX HORSEPOWER:
8.5 HP

LENGTH:
9 FT 2 IN (2.8 M)

WHEELBASE: 2 FT 8 IN (.82 M)

BULLDOZER

BULLDOZERS ARE USUALLY the first large machines to appear on a new work site, ripping up obstacles and pushing away the debris so other machines can do their work. The blade at the front can push over trees, level mounds, fill in hollows, and move piles of earth and rocks. The giant ripper at the back lives up to its name by tearing up the ground. Bulldozers can push scrapers out of trouble (see page 26), help move large pipes into position along a trench, and crunch through roads.

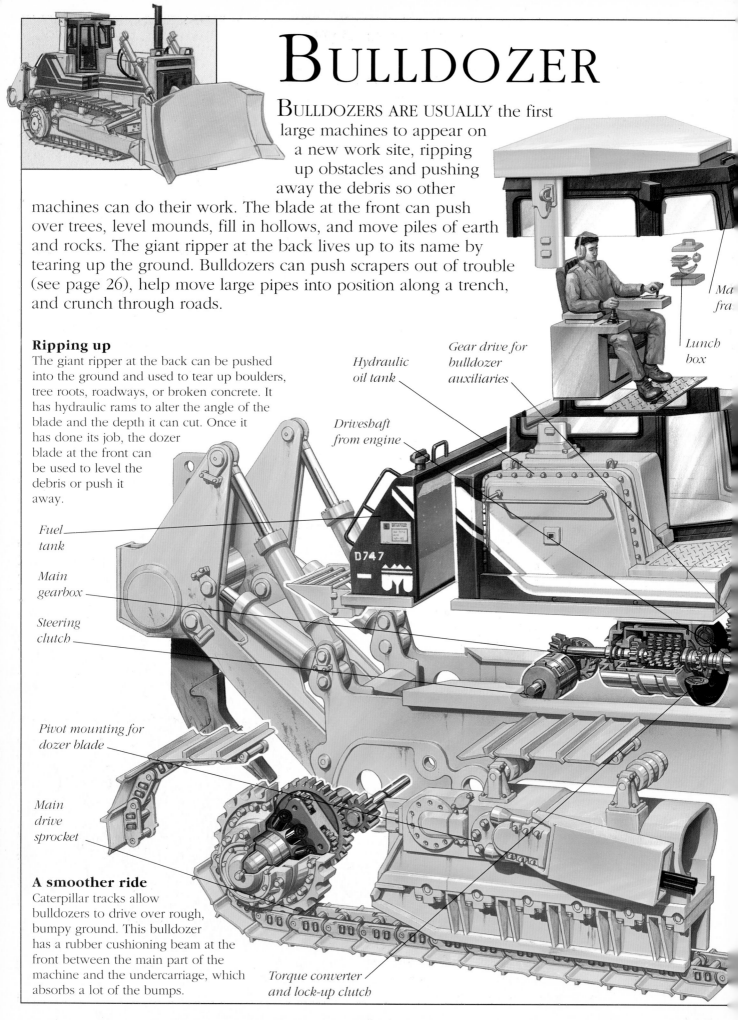

Ripping up
The giant ripper at the back can be pushed into the ground and used to tear up boulders, tree roots, roadways, or broken concrete. It has hydraulic rams to alter the angle of the blade and the depth it can cut. Once it has done its job, the dozer blade at the front can be used to level the debris or push it away.

Fuel tank

Main gearbox

Steering clutch

Pivot mounting for dozer blade

Main drive sprocket

A smoother ride
Caterpillar tracks allow bulldozers to drive over rough, bumpy ground. This bulldozer has a rubber cushioning beam at the front between the main part of the machine and the undercarriage, which absorbs a lot of the bumps.

Torque converter and lock-up clutch

Hydraulic oil tank

Driveshaft from engine

Gear drive for bulldozer auxiliaries

Ma fra

Lunch box

D747

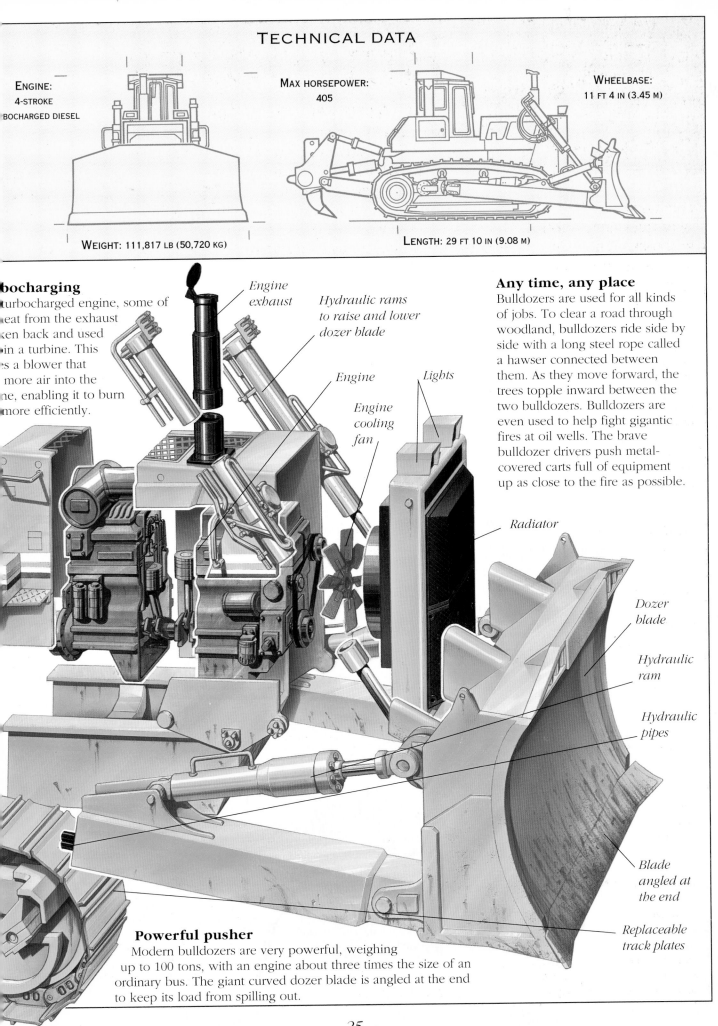

TECHNICAL DATA

ENGINE:
4-STROKE
BOCHARGED DIESEL

MAX HORSEPOWER:
405

WHEELBASE:
11 FT 4 IN (3.45 M)

WEIGHT: 111,817 LB (50,720 KG)

LENGTH: 29 FT 10 IN (9.08 M)

bocharging

urbocharged engine, some of
eat from the exhaust
ken back and used
in a turbine. This
s a blower that
more air into the
ne, enabling it to burn
more efficiently.

Engine
exhaust

Hydraulic rams
to raise and lower
dozer blade

Engine

Lights

Engine
cooling
fan

Any time, any place

Bulldozers are used for all kinds
of jobs. To clear a road through
woodland, bulldozers ride side by
side with a long steel rope called
a hawser connected between
them. As they move forward, the
trees topple inward between the
two bulldozers. Bulldozers are
even used to help fight gigantic
fires at oil wells. The brave
bulldozer drivers push metal-
covered carts full of equipment
up as close to the fire as possible.

Radiator

Dozer
blade

Hydraulic
ram

Hydraulic
pipes

Blade
angled at
the end

Replaceable
track plates

Powerful pusher

Modern bulldozers are very powerful, weighing
up to 100 tons, with an engine about three times the size of an
ordinary bus. The giant curved dozer blade is angled at the end
to keep its load from spilling out.

SCRAPER

ONCE A MAJOR ROAD HAS BEEN PLANNED, one of the first machines on the future road site will be a scraper. It can slice through earth and carry soil away, so it is ideal for leveling an area or for making slopes. First it slices layers from the ground and loads the loose soil into its basin. Once this is full, it will gradually unload the soil to fill hollows or pile it up to make embankments. When the scraper has finished, the outline of the new road will be clear, ready for the next phase of building.

Engine double-up
This machine has two engines. The one at the front drives the tractor part of the machine, where the driver sits. The one at the back drives the back wheels. However, even the most powerful scrapers frequently get stuck and need a bulldozer to push them out of trouble. The back of the scraper is reinforced to be strong enough to withstand a bulldozer pushing on it.

The cutting edge
To slice into the ground, the cutting edge is lowered and the apron, a metal flap above it, is raised. The cutter pushes into the earth for 12 in (300 mm) and then moves upward. The soil above it curls up like butter on a knife. It piles into the basin for storage, and the apron closes to trap it inside.

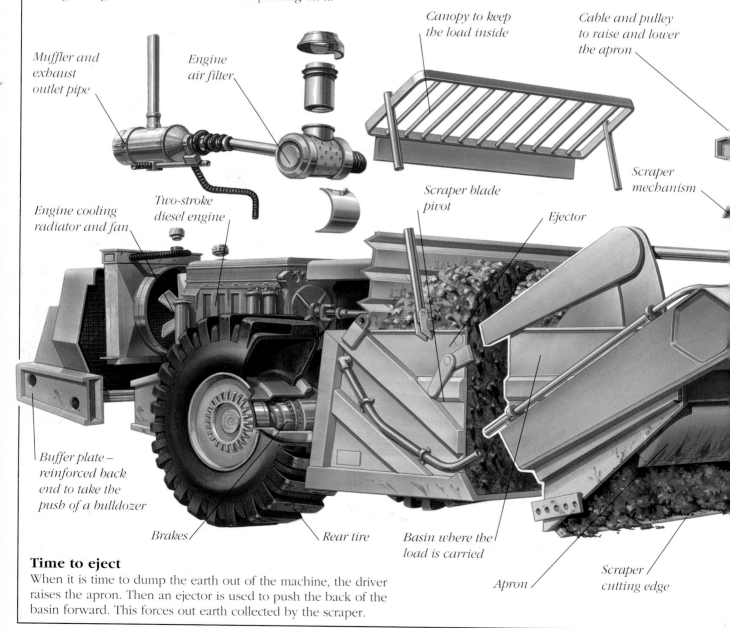

Muffler and exhaust outlet pipe

Engine air filter

Canopy to keep the load inside

Cable and pulley to raise and lower the apron

Engine cooling radiator and fan

Two-stroke diesel engine

Scraper blade pivot

Ejector

Scraper mechanism

Buffer plate – reinforced back end to take the push of a bulldozer

Brakes

Rear tire

Basin where the load is carried

Apron

Scraper cutting edge

Time to eject
When it is time to dump the earth out of the machine, the driver raises the apron. Then an ejector is used to push the back of the basin forward. This forces out earth collected by the scraper.

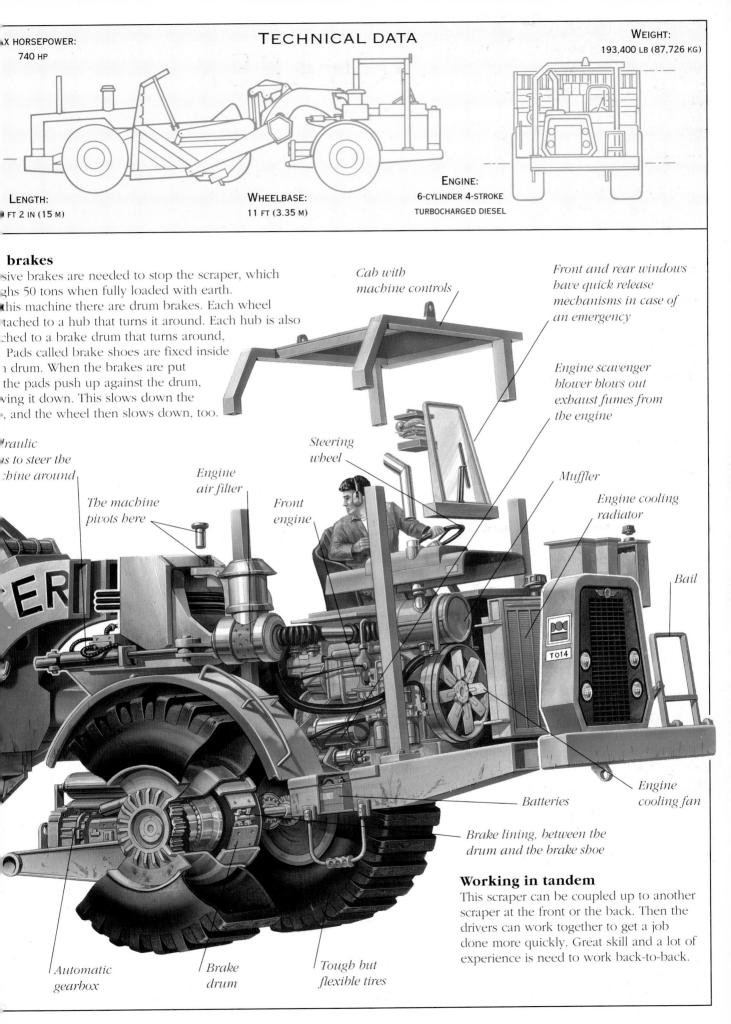

X HORSEPOWER:
740 HP

WEIGHT:
193,400 LB (87,726 KG)

LENGTH:
FT 2 IN (15 M)

WHEELBASE:
11 FT (3.35 M)

ENGINE:
6-CYLINDER 4-STROKE
TURBOCHARGED DIESEL

brakes

sive brakes are needed to stop the scraper, which
ghs 50 tons when fully loaded with earth.
this machine there are drum brakes. Each wheel
tached to a hub that turns it around. Each hub is also
ched to a brake drum that turns around,
Pads called brake shoes are fixed inside
drum. When the brakes are put
the pads push up against the drum,
ing it down. This slows down the
, and the wheel then slows down, too.

raulic
s to steer the
chine around

*The machine
pivots here*

*Engine
air filter*

*Cab with
machine controls*

*Steering
wheel*

*Front
engine*

*Front and rear windows
have quick release
mechanisms in case of
an emergency*

*Engine scavenger
blower blows out
exhaust fumes from
the engine*

Muffler

*Engine cooling
radiator*

Bail

*Engine
cooling fan*

Batteries

*Brake lining, between the
drum and the brake shoe*

*Automatic
gearbox*

*Brake
drum*

*Tough but
flexible tires*

Working in tandem

This scraper can be coupled up to another
scraper at the front or the back. Then the
drivers can work together to get a job
done more quickly. Great skill and a lot of
experience is need to work back-to-back.

HOW MACHINES WORK

THERE ARE LOTS OF DIFFERENT WORKING VEHICLES, but many of them have basic features in common. Here is a quick guide to some of the main features you have read about.

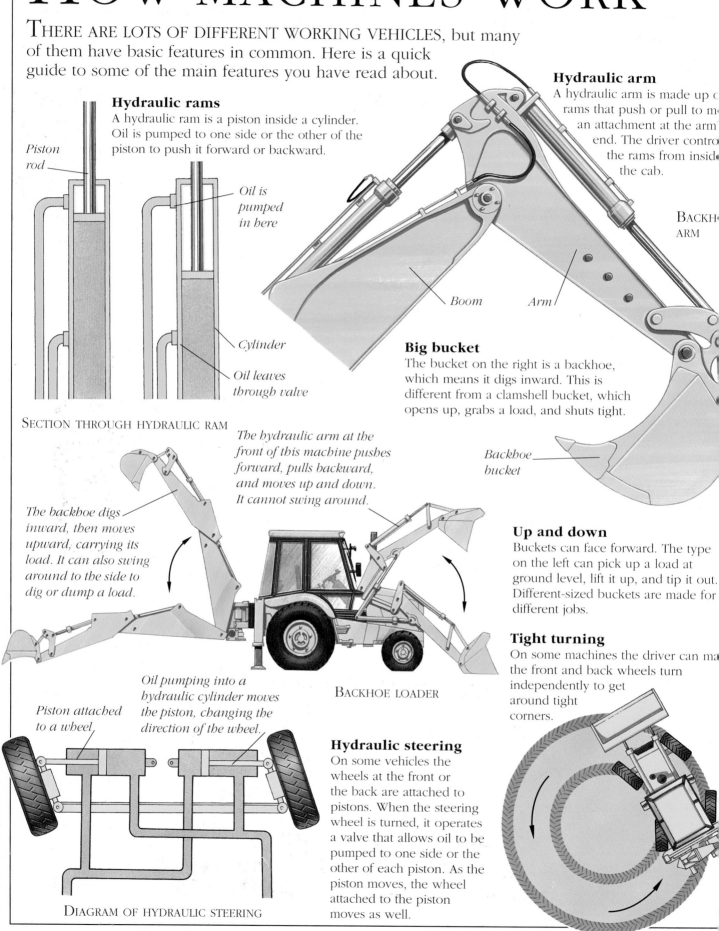

Hydraulic rams
A hydraulic ram is a piston inside a cylinder. Oil is pumped to one side or the other of the piston to push it forward or backward.

Piston rod

Oil is pumped in here

Cylinder

Oil leaves through valve

SECTION THROUGH HYDRAULIC RAM

Hydraulic arm
A hydraulic arm is made up of rams that push or pull to move an attachment at the arm's end. The driver controls the rams from inside the cab.

BACKHOE ARM

Boom

Arm

Big bucket
The bucket on the right is a backhoe, which means it digs inward. This is different from a clamshell bucket, which opens up, grabs a load, and shuts tight.

Backhoe bucket

The hydraulic arm at the front of this machine pushes forward, pulls backward, and moves up and down. It cannot swing around.

The backhoe digs inward, then moves upward, carrying its load. It can also swing around to the side to dig or dump a load.

BACKHOE LOADER

Up and down
Buckets can face forward. The type on the left can pick up a load at ground level, lift it up, and tip it out. Different-sized buckets are made for different jobs.

Tight turning
On some machines the driver can make the front and back wheels turn independently to get around tight corners.

Piston attached to a wheel

Oil pumping into a hydraulic cylinder moves the piston, changing the direction of the wheel.

Hydraulic steering
On some vehicles the wheels at the front or the back are attached to pistons. When the steering wheel is turned, it operates a valve that allows oil to be pumped to one side or the other of each piston. As the piston moves, the wheel attached to the piston moves as well.

DIAGRAM OF HYDRAULIC STEERING

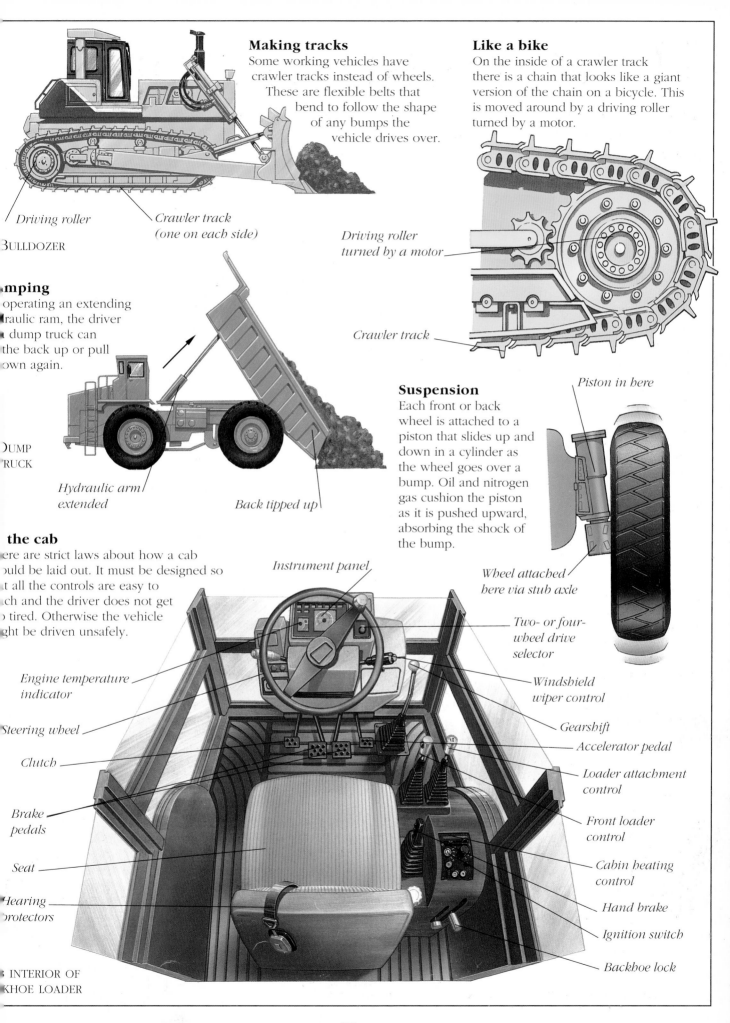

Making tracks

Some working vehicles have crawler tracks instead of wheels. These are flexible belts that bend to follow the shape of any bumps the vehicle drives over.

Like a bike

On the inside of a crawler track there is a chain that looks like a giant version of the chain on a bicycle. This is moved around by a driving roller turned by a motor.

Driving roller

*Crawler track
(one on each side)*

BULLDOZER

*Driving roller
turned by a motor*

Crawler track

..mping

..operating an extending
..raulic ram, the driver
.. dump truck can
.. the back up or pull
..own again.

DUMP
..RUCK

*Hydraulic arm
extended*

Back tipped up

Suspension

Each front or back wheel is attached to a piston that slides up and down in a cylinder as the wheel goes over a bump. Oil and nitrogen gas cushion the piston as it is pushed upward, absorbing the shock of the bump.

Piston in here

*Wheel attached
here via stub axle*

..the cab

..ere are strict laws about how a cab
..ould be laid out. It must be designed so
..t all the controls are easy to
..ch and the driver does not get
..o tired. Otherwise the vehicle
..ght be driven unsafely.

Instrument panel

*Two- or four-
wheel drive
selector*

*Engine temperature
indicator*

*Windshield
wiper control*

Steering wheel

Gearshift

Clutch

Accelerator pedal

*Loader attachment
control*

*Brake
pedals*

*Front loader
control*

Seat

*Cabin heating
control*

*Hearing
protectors*

Hand brake

Ignition switch

Backhoe lock

..INTERIOR OF
..KHOE LOADER

GLOSSARY

Air filter
This removes dirt from air before it goes into an engine.

Air horn
A loud horn fixed to a cab. Air is squeezed into the horn to make a warning noise.

Alternator
A part that makes electricity and puts it into a vehicle's battery. The alternator is driven by the engine.

Axle
A bar attaching a wheel to the main part of a vehicle. The power of the engine makes the axle spin, so the wheel spins around, too.

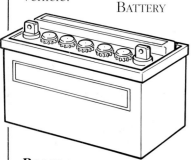

Gears

AXLE

Backhoe
A series of hydraulic arms with a bucket on the end, fitted to the back of a vehicle. It digs inward.

Battery
A part that provides and sends electricity to all the electrical systems of a vehicle.

BATTERY

Boom
The back part of a hydraulic arm. It raises

and lowers the front part, the head, which is usually attached to a bucket or grabber.

Bucket
A hydraulically operated scoop used for digging or loading.

Cab
The place where a driver sits and works the controls.

Canopy
A strong steel roof to protect a driver from flying stones.

Computer monitor
A series of sensors that measure the performance of a vehicle and send messages to an onboard computer. If the readings show a fault, the computer warns the driver.

Crankshaft
A part connected to an engine piston via thick rods. When the piston goes up and down, the crankshaft goes around, helping drive the wheels.

Crawler tracks
Wide flexible belts fitted to a vehicle instead of wheels. They go more smoothly over rough ground.

Differential
A part that allows the

wheels to turn around at different speeds, for instance when a vehicle turns a corner.

Disc brake
A metal disk that spins around together with a wheel. When the brake is used, the disk is squeezed between two pads, slowing the disk down, and thus the wheel.

Diesel engine
A series of cylinders with pistons inside. Fuel and air burn together in each cylinder, creating exhaust

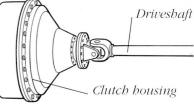

Driveshaft

Clutch housing

gases. The pistons move up and down, and the movement is used to drive the wheels.

Dozer blades
A wide curved blade fit at the front of a bulldoz and used for pushing o leveling.

Driveshaft
A part that helps transm the engine's power to the wheels.

Exhaust pipe
Exhaust gases go out in the air through this pipe

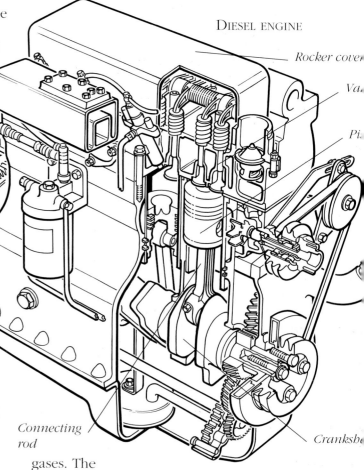

DIESEL ENGINE

Rocker cover

Va

Pi

Connecting rod

Crankshe

Fan (engine cooling)
This draws air through a radiator, cooling

water that passes
ough the radiator
route to and from
engine.

ur-wheel drive
ystem by which
four wheels on a
icle are driven
und by the power
he engine through
power train.

el tank
ontainer where fuel
tored
il it gets
d in the
gine.

arbox
is
luces

olutions
duced by
engine and
sses the power
to the wheels.

ad
e front part of a
draulic arm used
raise or lower a
bber or bucket.

aring protectors
muffs worn by
vers to cut out the
se of their vehicles.

draulic arm
et of hydraulic rams
d together and used
aise or lower a grabber
ucket.

draulic power pack
s contains all
hydraulic pumps
valves needed
operating the
raulics on a
icle.

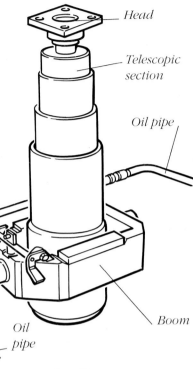

HYDRAULIC
RAM

Head

*Telescopic
section*

Oil pipe

*Oil
pipe*

Boom

Hydraulic ram
A piston inside a cylinder.
Oil is pumped to one side
or the other of a piston
to push it forward or
backward. This moves any
parts attached to
the ram.

Oil-cooled
When a component is
fitted inside a container
of oil to cool working
parts.

Oil filter
A fine gauze that filters
dirt out of oil before it
gets into hydraulic parts.

Piston
The part that goes up and
down inside a hydraulic
cylinder or engine cylinder.

Power train
All the parts that transmit
power from the engine
through to the wheels.

Radiator
Hot water
from the
engine is
pumped
through the
tubes in a
radiator to
be cooled
before it
returns to
the engine.

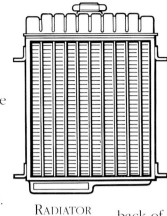

RADIATOR

Ripper
A giant pointed cutter
fitted to the back of a
bulldozer and used
for ripping up ground.

Roller
A round part fitted in
the middle of a crawler
track. The biggest one,
the driving roller, is
driven around by a motor.
The other smaller rollers
follow, moving the
track along as they turn.

Stabilizer
A hydraulically operated
leg that extends from a
chassis to help keep it
steady.

Suspension
Parts designed to absorb
the shock of bumps as a
vehicle travels
over bumpy
ground.

SUSPENSION

*Shock
absorber*

*Wheel
hub*

Swinging gear
A big gear unit
that can swing
a cab around if
the driver wants
to dig or dump a
load in a different
position.

Tipping body
A strong steel
container at the
back of a dump truck. A
hydraulic ram tips it up to
pour out a load.

Torque
The work that an engine
piston does to turn a
crankshaft. The more
powerful the engine, the
more torque it produces.

Tread
The pattern on the
outside of a tire. It varies
depending on the job to
be done.

Turbocharging
When some of the heat
produced by an engine
is used to drive a blower
that puts more air into
the engine, making it
more powerful.

Two-wheel drive
A system by which only
one set of wheels is
driven by the power of
the engine.

Valve
A part that opens and
closes to let oil through
to different parts of a
hydraulic system.

Wheel hub
The part that a wheel
is fitted to. A hub, in
turn, is attached to a
wheel axle.

INDEX

A

air horns, 9
apron, 26
augers, 12, 13

B

backhoe, 20, 28
backhoe loader, 20-21
basin, 26
battery, 15, 27, 30
boom, 7, 10, 14, 15, 18,
    19, 20, 21, 22, 21,
    23, 28, 30
brake shoes, 27
brakes, 7, 8, 15, 17, 21, 24,
    26, 27, 15, 27
buckets, 28, 29
    backhoe loader,
        20, 21, 23, 28
    excavator, 19
    mining shovel, 10
    skid steer, 22
    wheel loader, 6, 7
bulldozer, 24-25

C

Cabs, 6, 9, 11, 14, 15, 17,
    18, 20, 22, 24, 27,
    29
cement mixer, 16-17
chassis, 17
computer system, 11, 30
crawler tracks, 11, 23, 29
cutter, 26

D

diesel engine, 6, 9, 11, 13,
    14, 15, 17, 21, 23,
    26, 30
disc brakes, 7, 15, 20, 21
dozer blade, 23, 24, 25
dredging bucket, 19
driveshafts, 22

driving sprocket, 29
drum, 16, 17
drum brakes, 27
dump truck, 8-9, 13, 29
dumping, 29

E

ejector, 26
engine cooling system, 9
engines, 6, 14, 25
    bulldozer, 25
    cement mixer, 16
    excavator, 18
    scraper, 26
    truck crane, 14
excavator, 18-19
    mini-, 23
exhaust fumes, 13

F

feeders, 13
flights, 16
forklift, 22
four-wheel drive, 20

G

grabber, 18, 19
grapples, 19

H

hawser, 25
head, 19, 29
hearing protectors, 23
hydraulic
    arm, 28
    power pack, 18
    ram, 7, 9, 10, 15,
        18, 19, 28, 20, 22,
        23, 25, 27, 28, 31
    steering, 27, 28
hydraulics, 28, 30

L

loaders, 6

M

mini-excavator, 23
mining shovel, 10-11

R

radiator, 9, 14, 17, 18, 21,
    25, 26, 27, 31
ripper, 24
roller vehicle, 12

S

scraper, 26-27
screed plates, 12, 13
skid steer, 22
spreading vehicle, 12
stabilizers, 15
steering, 6, 7, 13, 14, 17,
    20, 21, 24, 25, 27,
    28, 29;
see also wheels
suspension, 9, 14, 15, 29,
    31
swinging gear, 11, 15, 18,
    23, 31

T

teeth, 7, 10, 19, 20, 21, 22,
    23
telescopic boom see boom
tipping body, 8
tires, 6, 9, 13, 15, 18, 22,
    26, 27
torque, 14, 31
track paver, 12-13
transmission gearbox, 9,
    24, 27
truck crane, 14-15
turbocharged engine, 25,
    27
two-wheel drive, 9, 31

W

wheel loader, 6-7
wheeled excavator,
    18-19
wheels, 28
    cement mixer, 16,
        17
    dump truck, 9
    skid steer, 22
    track paver, 12, 13
    truck crane, 15
    wheel loader, 7

Acknowledgments

Dorling Kindersley would
like to thank the following
people who helped in the
preparation of this book:
Lynn Bresler for the index
Helen Baxter, J.C.B.,
Ian Vickerstaff, Terex Ltd
Barber Greene,
Benford,
J.I. Case International,
Caterpillar Inc.,
Edbro,
Foden,
Komatsu,
Orenstein and Koppel,
Tadano-Faun,
Volvo.